Animal Lives

PENGUINS

Sally Morgan

D1254562

QEB Publishing

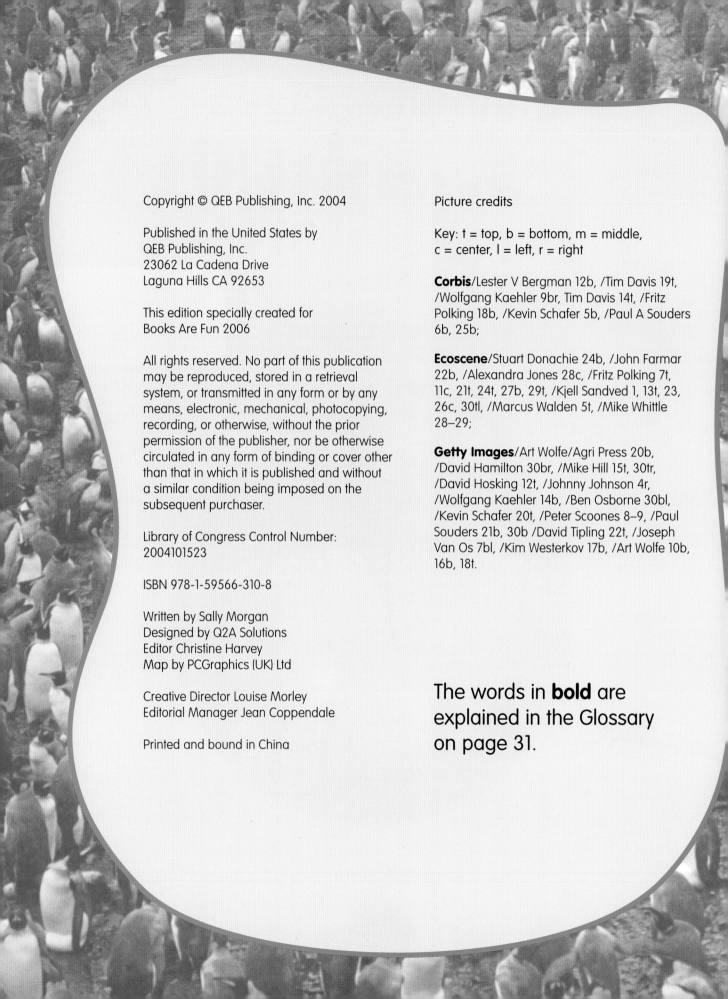

Published in the United States by
QEB Publishing, Inc.
23062 La Cadena Drive
Laguna Hills CA 92653

This edition specially created for
Books Are Fun 2006

Library of Congress Control Number:
2004101523

ISBN 978-1-59566-310-8

Written by Sally Morgan
Designed by Q2A Solutions
Editor Christine Harvey
Map by PCGraphics (UK) Ltd

Creative Director Louise Morley
Editorial Manager Jean Coppendale

Printed and bound in China

The words in **bold** are
explained in the Glossary
on page 31.

Contents

The penguin 4
Types of penguins 6
Where do you find penguins? 8
Living in colonies 10
Laying eggs 12
Growing up 14
Laying eggs—Emperor penguins 16
Growing up—Emperor penguins 18
Walking and swimming 20
Penguin food 22
Penguin predators 24
Keeping warm 26
Penguins under threat 28
Life cycle 30
Glossary 31
Index 32

The penguin

It is easy to recognize a penguin, with its black back and white front. Penguins are plump, with short legs and **webbed** feet.

Penguins belong to a group of animals called birds. Birds are covered in feathers and they reproduce by laying eggs. Most birds have front limbs that are **adapted** to form wings.

These King penguins have a black back and a white front.

4

Adélie penguins have a white ring around each eye. They have a short beak, partly covered by feathers.

Penguin

- Most penguins live between ten and fifteen years.
- Emperor penguins can live up to twenty-five years.

facts

The smallest type of penguins are called Little penguins!

How penguins move

Most birds use their wings to fly. But the penguin is different from other birds because it can't fly. However, it is an excellent swimmer and can even sleep on water!

Birds stand on their back legs. The penguin is unusual because it stands very upright. When a penguin walks, it **waddles** from side-to-side.

Types of penguins

The King penguin has an orange teardrop at the side of its head. The Emperor penguin has a yellow one.

There are seventeen species, or types, of penguin. The largest are the Emperor and the King penguins, which look very similar.

Penguin facts

• The Emperor penguin is 4 feet tall and weighs 65 to 85 pounds – the size of a child.
• The Little penguin stands just 14 to 16 inches high and weighs around 2 pounds.

Crested penguins

Six species have a crest of feathers on top of their heads and are called crested penguins. They are the Erect-crested, Fiordland, Macaroni, Rockhopper, Royal and Snares penguins. The largest of the crested penguins is the Macaroni penguin.

The Chinstrap penguin is named after the thin black line running under its chin.

The Macaroni penguin has a crest of yellow feathers on its head.

Other penguins

There are eight other species of penguin. They are the Adélie, African, Chinstrap, Galapagos, Gentoo, Humboldt, Magellanic and Yellow-eyed penguins. Gentoo penguins look like they have a white bonnet on their heads. While Humboldt penguins have a white stripe across their heads.

7

Where do you find penguins?

Many people think that penguins only live in the coldest parts of the world. However, only two species of penguin, the Adélie and the Emperor, live in the Antarctic all year round. Many species of penguin only visit Antarctica in the summer, when it is not as cold.

Emperor penguins are found in Antartica all year round. They can survive the long, cold winter.

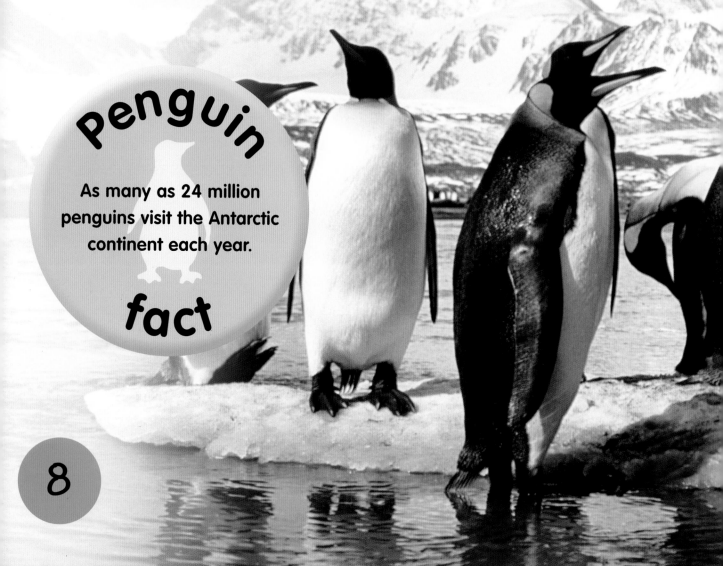

Penguin
As many as 24 million penguins visit the Antarctic continent each year.

fact

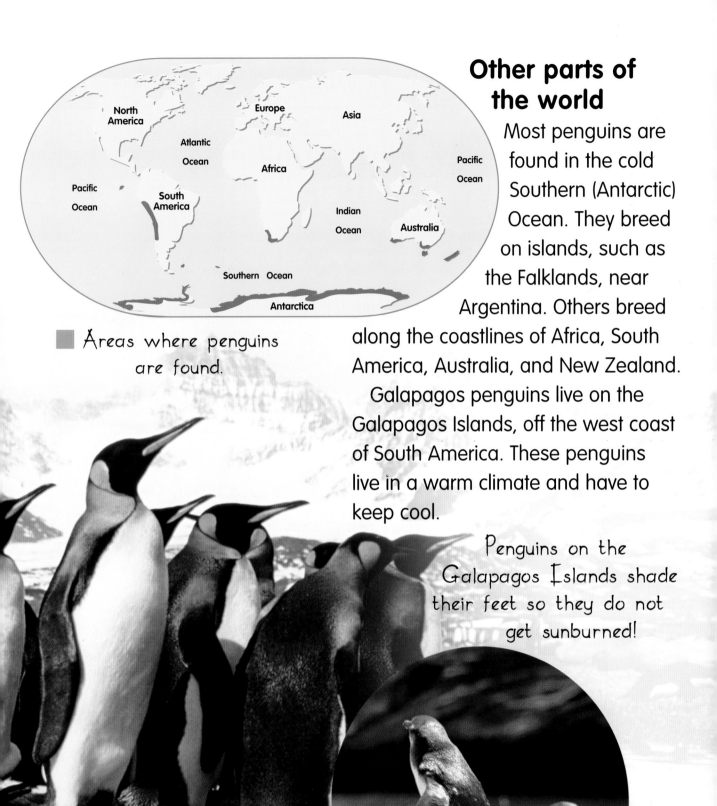

Other parts of the world

Most penguins are found in the cold Southern (Antarctic) Ocean. They breed on islands, such as the Falklands, near Argentina. Others breed along the coastlines of Africa, South America, Australia, and New Zealand. Galapagos penguins live on the Galapagos Islands, off the west coast of South America. These penguins live in a warm climate and have to keep cool.

North America

Europe

Asia

Atlantic Ocean

Africa

Pacific Ocean

Pacific Ocean

South America

Indian Ocean

Australia

Southern Ocean

Antarctica

Areas where penguins are found.

Penguins on the Galapagos Islands shade their feet so they do not get sunburned!

9

Living in colonies

Penguins like to be close to other penguins. When they are on land, penguins live together in large groups called colonies. Colonies vary in size and can have 400 or 40,000 penguins in them. There are about forty different Emperor penguin colonies in the Antarctic.

A huge colony of King penguins.

A place in the colony

Penguins come onto land at the beginning of the mating season. Each pair of penguins has its own space in the colony. This is where they make their nest. They will chase away other penguins that come too close to their nest.

Adélie penguin colonies are usually large with hundreds of thousands of individual birds.

Laying eggs

Penguins come onto land to mate and breed. Most penguins lay their eggs in a simple nest made of feathers, grass, or even a pile of rocks. The African, Humboldt, Magellanic, Galapagos, and Little penguins lay their eggs in burrows. They use their beaks to dig out the burrows.

Penguins return to the same place each year to breed.

Incubating the eggs

Penguins only lay one or two eggs. The eggs are **incubated** by both parents. They take turns looking after the eggs over a period of about two months.

Penguins have to keep their egg warm throughout the incubation period.

Penguin fact

Of the two eggs laid by penguins, often only one chick hatches. Sometimes both hatch but only one survives.

Hatching

Once the chick is ready to hatch, it chips its way out of the shell using an egg-tooth on the end of its beak.

Growing up

A newly hatched chick nestles under its parent to keep warm. One parent stays with the chick while the other feeds in the sea. Older chicks are left in **kindergarten** groups while both their parents feed. Leaving the chicks in a group provides more protection from **predators** and from the cold.

Adult penguins will only recognize and feed their own chicks.

A penguin kindergarten can be very large with many hundreds of chicks tightly packed together.

14

Growing adult feathers

Penguin chicks have fluffy feathers that trap heat and help keep them warm. As they get older, these feathers are replaced by adult feathers. This takes between seven and ten weeks.

The adult feathers are **waterproof**. This means that penguins do not have to dry their feathers when they come out of the sea. The fluffy chick feathers are not waterproof, so penguin chicks can't go into the water until they have grown their adult feathers.

King penguin chicks have brown fluffy feathers. They look very different from their parents.

Penguin

Early explorers thought that King penguin chicks, with their fluffy brown feathers, were a separate species and called them Wooly penguins!

fact

Laying eggs– Emperor penguins

Emperor penguins live in the Antarctic all year round. They lay their eggs in the middle of winter.

The penguins walk inland to their breeding site, called a rookery. The female lays one egg and passes it to the male. The male penguin places the egg on his feet and covers it with a flap of skin to keep it warm. The female penguin returns to the ocean for two months to feed, leaving the male with the egg.

Emperor penguins start their long walk inland in the middle of winter.

Keeping warm

The male penguins huddle together in a group to keep warm. They shuffle forward all the time, taking turns to walk to the outside of the huddle where it's the coldest. They do not eat while they are **incubating** an egg, and can lose up to 45 percent of their body weight.

Penguin fact

Emperor penguins do not make nests. They keep their egg warm by balancing it on top of their feet.

As many as 6,000 male Emperor penguins will huddle together while incubating their eggs.

17

Growing up–
Emperor penguins

The Emperor penguin chick hatches two months after laying. The chick needs food, so the male regurgitates (brings up) food from his stomach to feed it. Then the female penguin returns from the ocean and takes over. The male walks slowly back to the water to feed.

Penguin

If the female does not return from the ocean, the male abandons his egg or chick and walks back to the water. If he stays with the chick, he will die of starvation.

fact

During the summer months the parents take turns caring for their chick.

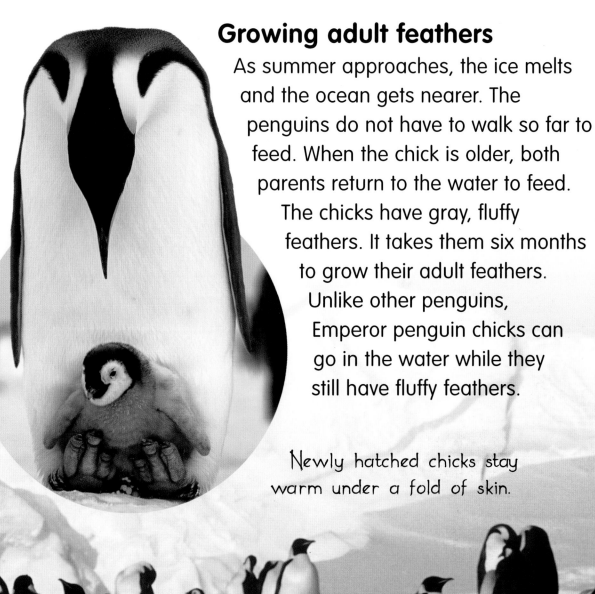

Growing adult feathers

As summer approaches, the ice melts and the ocean gets nearer. The penguins do not have to walk so far to feed. When the chick is older, both parents return to the water to feed. The chicks have gray, fluffy feathers. It takes them six months to grow their adult feathers. Unlike other penguins, Emperor penguin chicks can go in the water while they still have fluffy feathers.

Newly hatched chicks stay warm under a fold of skin.

19

Walking and swimming

The penguin's body is **streamlined**, and is the perfect design for swimming. Penguins use their wings like flippers to swim through the water. Their **webbed** feet act like paddles when floating on the surface, and as rudders for steering when the penguins are underwater. Penguins have heavy bones to help them stay underwater.

Penguins leap into, and out of, the water.

In water and on land

Once young penguins have their adult feathers they can learn to swim. At first they return to land each night, but soon they spend most of their time in the water. During their first few years, they grow and put on fat before returning to land to breed.

Penguins **waddle** on land. They look clumsy, but their waddle saves energy and helps keep them warm.

Sometimes Penguins "toboggan" on their fronts over snow and ice, pushing with their feet and flippers.

Penguins walk by swinging one leg forward and then the next. They rock from side-to-side as they walk.

21

Penguin food

Penguins feed mostly on fish, squid, and **krill**. Each penguin species has a beak designed to catch its **prey**. King penguins have a long, curved beak, which is ideal for catching large squid. The Humboldt penguin has a short, thick beak for catching small fish, such as sardines and anchovies.

Many penguins feed on krill.

The King penguin has a much longer, thinner beak than other penguins.

Hunting

Most penguins feed during the day. They have two ways of hunting. Sometimes they swim under the ice to find shoals of fish and krill. They also dive deep to catch squid and deep-sea fish.

Like other penguins, the Gentoo brings up food from its stomach to feed its chick.

Feeding chicks

Penguin chicks ask for food by pecking at the base of their parents' beaks. This makes the parent regurgitate a meal from its stomach. When they have their adult feathers, young penguins can catch food for themselves.

23

Penguin predators

Penguins are hunted by sea animals, such as sharks, leopard seals, and killer whales. Young penguins are at risk in the water, especially when they go into the ocean for the first time. **Predators** gather close to the beaches where young penguins enter the water. The young penguins have to learn quickly how to avoid predators. Many penguins die during their first few months in the ocean.

The fierce Leopard seal is a predator of penguins.

Air and land predators

Seabirds, such as skuas, gulls, and giant petrels, swoop down and attack young penguin chicks.

Penguins that live on **inhabited** islands have other types of predators. Dogs, cats, rats, and weasels kill the smaller species of penguins, and take their eggs and chicks.

penguin

When a penguin is swimming on the surface, its white front blends with the sunlight, making it difficult for predators to see the penguin from below. Its black back blends with the dark water, making it difficult for predators to spot it from above.

fact

Skuas also steal and eat penguin eggs.

Keeping warm

Penguins are **adapted** to the cold. Their body is covered in feathers. Beneath their skin they have a thick layer of fat called blubber. This traps heat in their body and stops it escaping. When penguins swim, their muscles release heat and this helps keep their bodies warm in cold water.

Feathers and fat help keep the penguin warm.

Surviving the first winter

Penguins have specially adapted blood vessels in their feet. These supply just enough heat to prevent their feet freezing to the ice.

Penguin chicks have to grow quickly. They need to be large enough, and have enough fat, to survive their first winter.

Penguin

Penguins can survive in temperatures well below freezing (32°F).

fact

Emperor penguins have to survive the strong winds and blizzards of the Antarctic.

Penguins under threat

Penguins living on islands that are **inhabited** by humans are often killed by animals, such as dogs and cats. Conservation organizations are trying to protect penguins by removing these predators from the islands.

These Little penguins were rescued after an oil spill. Volunteers have cleaned their feathers and soon they will be released back into the ocean.

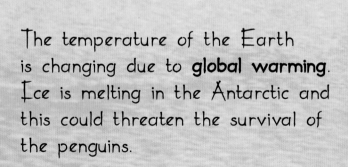

The temperature of the Earth is changing due to **global warming**. Ice is melting in the Antarctic and this could threaten the survival of the penguins.

Other threats

People are **overfishing** many of the world's oceans. Too many fish are taken and this means that there is less food left for penguins. Overfishing could be stopped by new international laws that would control the quantities of fish caught by fishermen.

Oil spills at sea also affect penguins. Oil sticks to the penguins' feathers, making them less waterproof. It also reduces the warmth that the penguins are able to trap next to their skin. While trying to clean their feathers, the penguins swallow the oil, which can poison them or cause damage to their internal organs.

This King penguin is covered in oil after swimming through an oil spill in the Southern Ocean.

penguin

The Yellow-eyed and Peruvian penguins are the rarest types. They are classed as endangered because they may become extinct soon.

fact

29

Life cycle of a penguin

Penguins come onto land to mate and lay their eggs. The eggs are **incubated** for two months. The chicks are born with fluffy feathers. Young penguins are fed by their parents.

Once they have grown their adult **waterproof** feathers, penguins can go to the ocean. They stay at sea feeding and growing for many months.

An egg ready to hatch.

A one-month-old chick

Six-month-old chicks

Four-year-old penguins

Glossary

adapted changed to suit the environment they live in

global warming warming of the planet due to holes in the ozone layer of Earth's atmosphere

incubate to keep eggs warm so the chicks inside will grow

inhabited lived in, occupied

kindergarten a day nursery for penguin chicks

krill penguin food, such as small shrimp and plankton

overfishing taking too many fish from the sea

predator an animal that hunts and eats other animals

prey an animal that is hunted by another animal

streamlined having a smooth, bullet shape that slips easily through the water

waddle to sway from side to side while walking

waterproof not allowing water to pass through

webbed having thin flaps of skin between the toes of the feet

Index

adaptation 4, 26, 31
Adélie penguins 5, 7, 11
African penguins 7, 12
Antarctic 8, 28

beaks 5, 12, 13, 22
birds 4
blood vessels 27
blubber 26
bones 20
breeding 12–13, 16–17
burrows 12

chicks 14–15, 18–19,
    27, 30
    feeding 18, 23, 30
Chinstrap penguins 7, 10
colonies 10–11
coloring 4, 25
conservation 28
Crested penguins 7

diving 23

egg-laying 12–13, 16–17
egg-tooth 13
Emperor penguins 5, 6,
    8, 10, 16–19, 23, 27
endangered species 29
Erect-crested penguins 7

fat 26
feathers 4, 15, 19, 26,
    30
    feet 4, 20, 27, 31

Fiordland penguins 7
food 22–3

Galapagos Islands 9
Galapagos penguins 7,
    9, 12
Gentoo penguins 7, 23
global warming 28, 31
growing up 14–15, 18–19

hatching 13, 18, 30
height 6
Humboldt penguins 7,
    12, 22
hunting 23

incubation 13, 31
inhabited islands 25, 28,
    31

keeping warm 26–27
Kindergarten 14, 31
King penguins 4, 6, 10,
    15, 22, 29
krill 22, 31

legs 4
Leopard seals 24
life cycle 30
life span 5
Little penguins 5, 12, 28

Macaroni penguins 7
Magellanic penguins 7,
    12
males:
    feeding chicks 18
    incubating eggs 13,
    16–17

mating 11, 12, 30
moving 5

nests 11, 12

oil spills 28, 29
overfishing 29, 31

Peruvian penguins 29
predators 14, 24–25, 31
prey 22, 31

Rockhopper penguins 7
rookery 16
Royal penguins 7

sleeping 5
Snares penguins 7
species 6–7
streamlining 20, 31
sunburn 9
swimming 5, 20–21, 26

threats to penguins
    28–29
tobogganing 21

waddling 5, 21, 31
walking 5, 20, 21
waterproof 15, 29, 30, 31
webbed feet 4, 20, 31
weight 6, 17
wings 4, 5, 20

Yellow-eyed penguins 7,
    29